Drawing
ANIMALS

By
Rajni & Ajay

UNICORN BOOKS

ISBN: 978-81-7806-130-6 © Publishers
Drawing Animals
UNICORN BOOKS Pvt. Ltd., F-2/16, Ansari Road,
Darya Ganj, New Delhi-110002
Phones: 011-23262683, 23250704, Fax: 23257790
E-mail: info@unicornbooks.in
Website: www.unicornbooks.in

Contents

Cat

Monkeys

Saki Monkey

Introduction

Nature has provided a fascinating atmosphere and surrounding for humans to live in.

Animals are an inseparable part of our existence. Try to grasp the basic nature of the animal you are drawing. Weight and volume of the animal is also important. Its skin and body type is the third thing to keep in mind. Last and the most important thing we generally miss is the atmosphere and background in which we put an animal.

Just keep these four points at the back of your mind and go through this book, drawing everything which comes in your way. We assure you, you will find a big change in your artistic talents by the time you reach the last page.

The Basic Structure

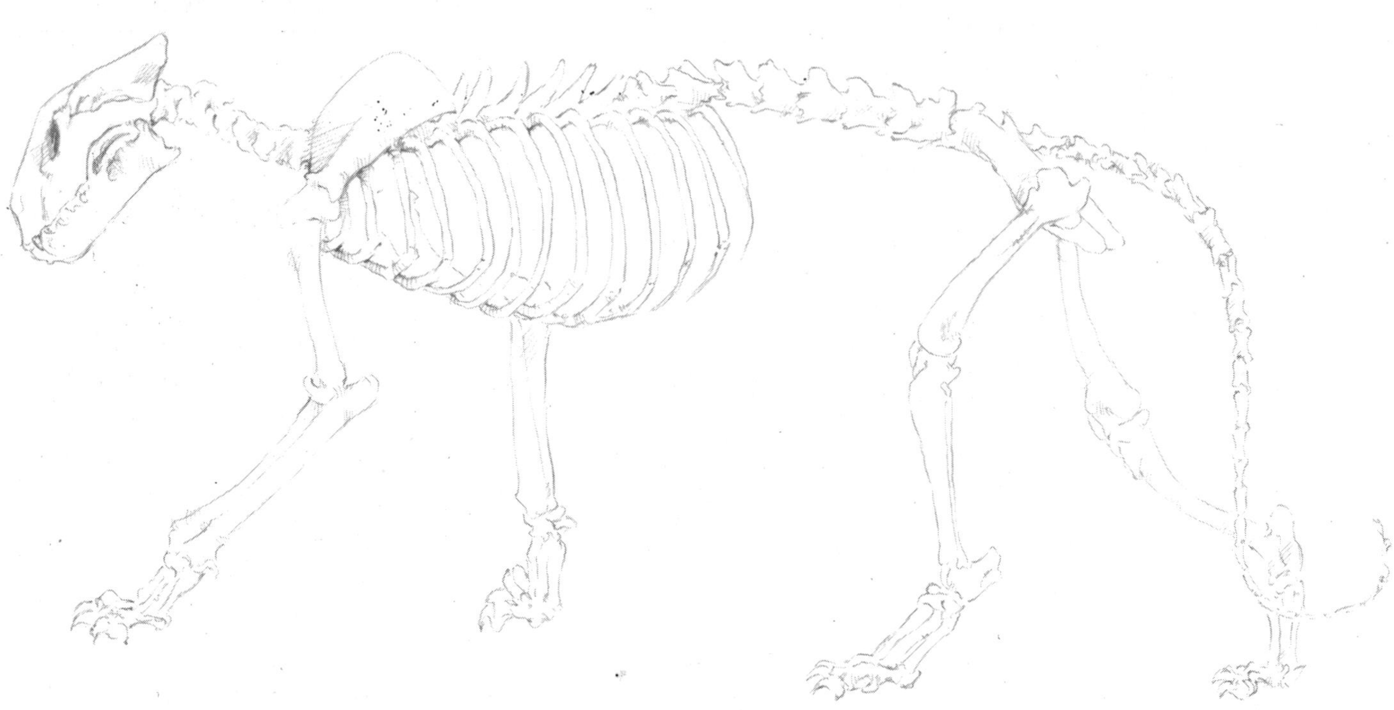

When you start drawing an animal you must know about the shape you want to achieve. It is like making something from the wheat flour dough as a five-year old will do. You should know the underlying frame on which you will develop the ultimate shape of the animal concerned.

Study the bone structure, the big and small muscles of your animal, whenever you get the chance. Apart from recording the proportions and main parts, see how it moves. The body keeps changing its shape as it moves.

After placing the basic structure, work on the outer look of the animal. Type of skin and the texture plays a very crucial role in the ultimate appearance of the creature. Always work on a small part as if it is a separate section. This approach is very effective when you are creating the fine details, small interrelating shades and shadows or the slight curves of the planes of the body.

Lion

Look at the final picture above and the primary stages on the opposite page. Try to draw the Lion directly first and then by going through the two primary stages. Do not draw the bones and muscles as fine as given here. Just mark it boldly but in a very light tone. Now draw the final picture on this base. Even only one exercise of this type will make you see the difference this knowledge can create.

Lion

Sitting and lying posture of various animals are very different. Nature and basic traits are important here.

Look at this Lion relaxing peacefully on a warm day. The head should be bigger than the corresponding body so the perspective of its projection towards you can be created.

Lion

Facial expressions of an animal in different moods and situations should also be recorded. An angry Lion has small eyes, widely open mouth and big teeth, as you can see on the opposite page.

Now see a different mood when it is having a nap. Eyes are also small here but the other muscles of the face are totally relaxed and inactive.

The Strokes

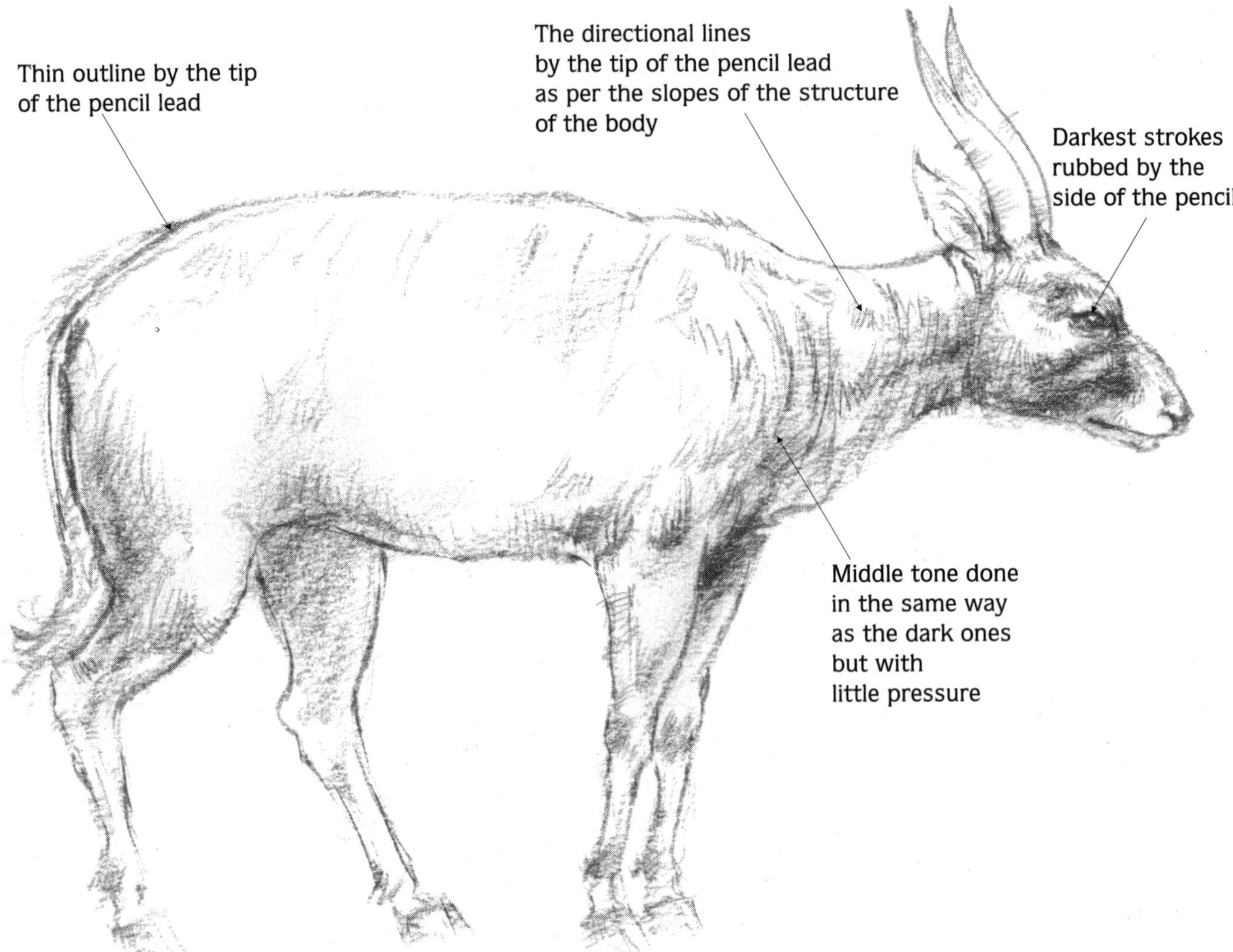

Bongo

To achieve the correct texture of the skin, we use various types of strokes. Look and observe the selection and resulting outcome of a stroke. Co-relate it with the area of application and try to reason out the choice.

See the Bongo here, outline of the body is finished in light and thin lines. Then the shadows on and under the body are done in broad strokes. The darkest shades are on the face, between the front legs and in the eyes. Also note the direction, originating and ending points of a stroke. A stroke's direction is the deciding factor in defining the curvature of the body.

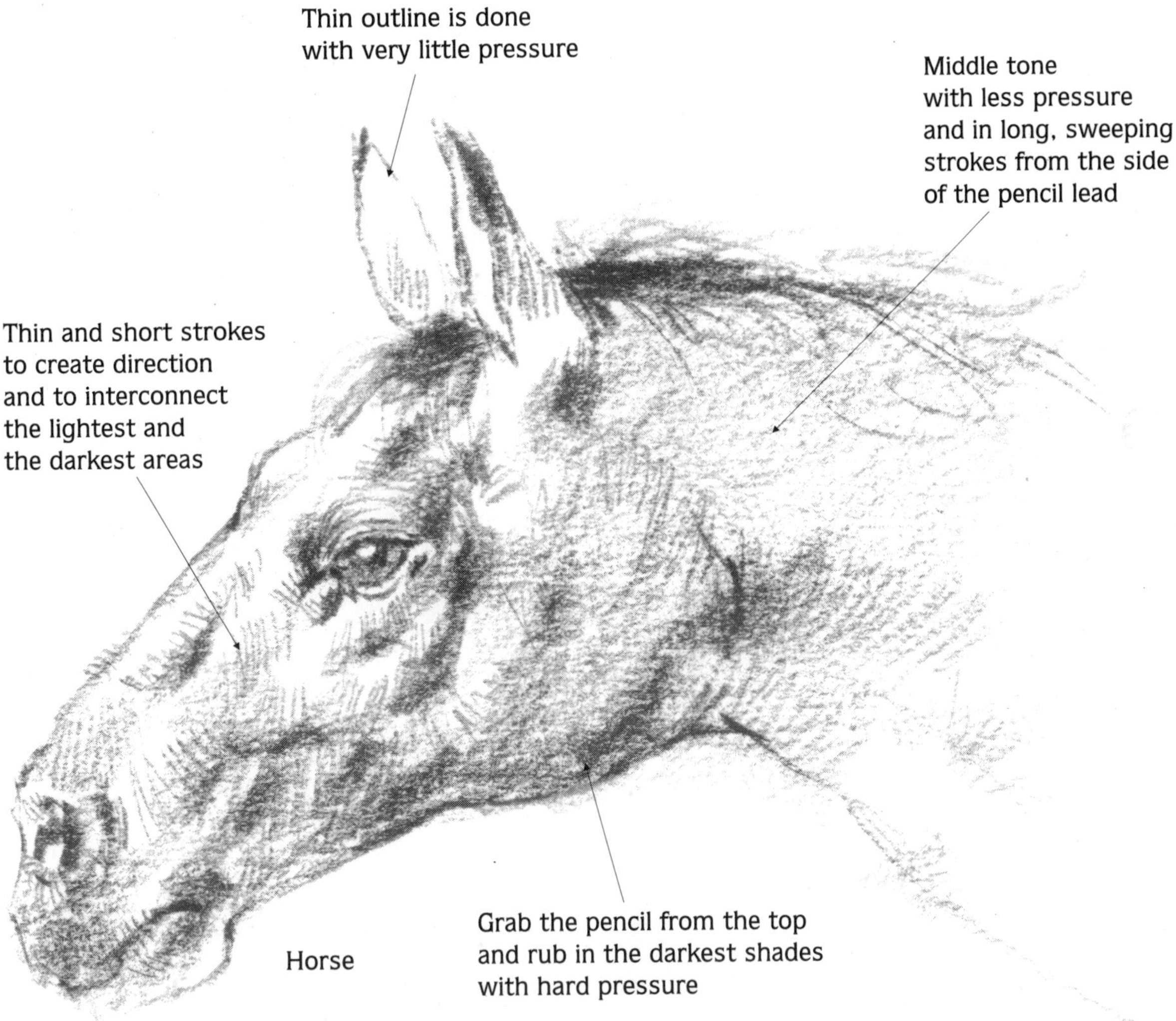

Horse

Look at the picture you are going to draw very closely and attentively. Decide beforehand where you want to put heaviness and weight. We have used light and thin lines to draw the outline of the horse. As the light is coming from the top left side, the darker areas will fall on the right and bottom side. After drawing the outline we have rubbed in the darkest parts using the side of the pencil lead. The middle tone is again placed in the same fashion but with little pressure to create a lighter tone. Now comes the role of the directional strokes. You can see these tiny, thin lines on the neck, lower jaw, around the eyes and at the side of upper jaw.

Rabbits

Rabbits are small, soft, whitish and agile animals. Stick to light and fewer strokes. Use directional ones as much as possible.

Look at the sketch on the left side. Only the eyes and the area between the front legs has some dark shades. We have left even the light-middle tones and focussed on the parts where the shades have become very pronounced.

After doing the outline as a whole we have placed the darkest tones on eyes and other areas first. Other lines are only those which were obsolutely necessary.

Rabbits

Drawing the same animal from different angles is always an excellent way to get command on its postures and body movements. Do not finish the whole picture, instead, concentrate on the focal point like head in the example given below. Accurate and flexible lines are the essence of this type of sketch.

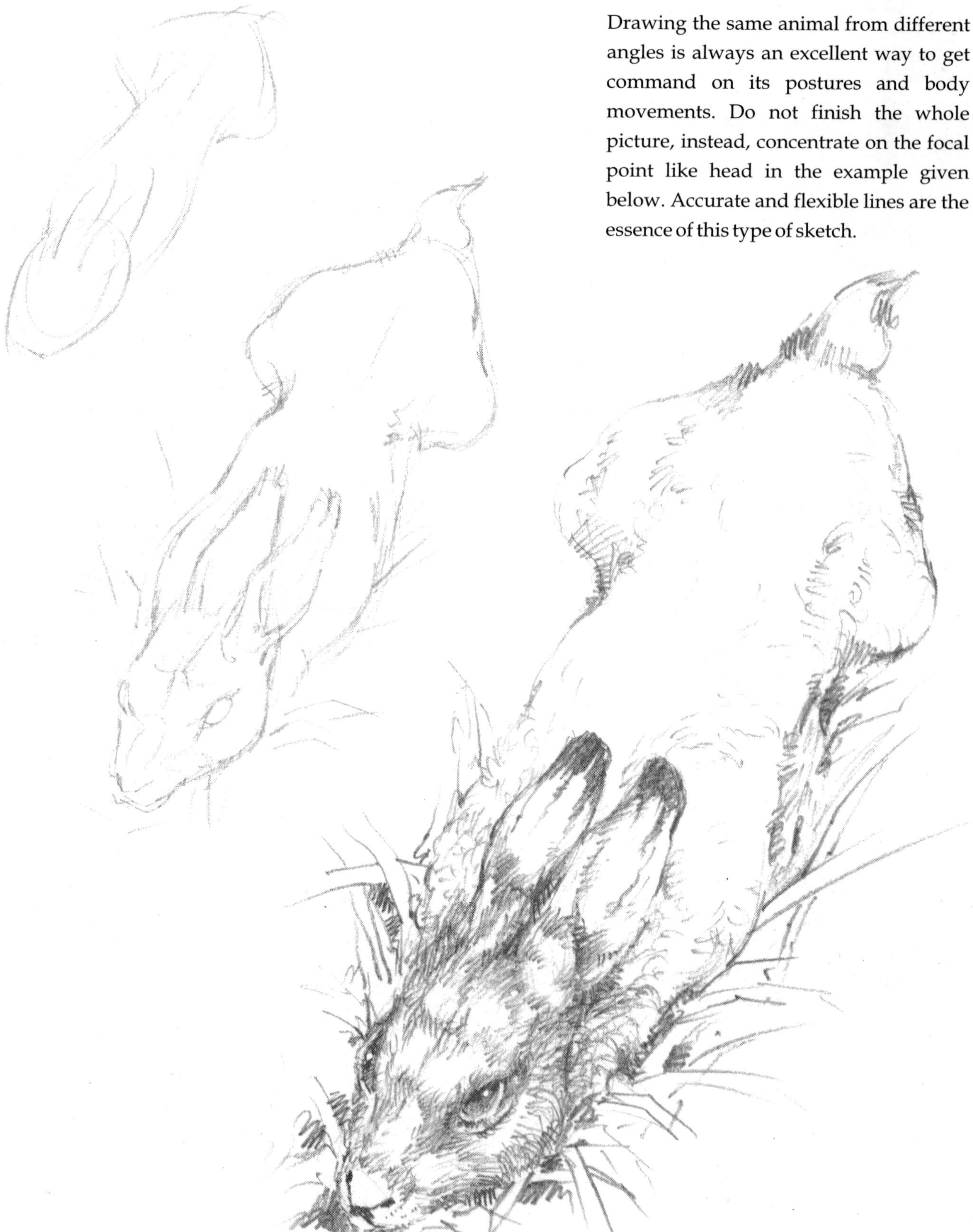

Rabbits

Can you see what is special in the portrait given here? We have applied some straight and thick strokes but in middle tone to create background. Same type of lines have been used on the upper parts of the neck and the head. This act has connected the Rabbit with the background. When studying an animal for oil painting, this type of exercise is very helpful.

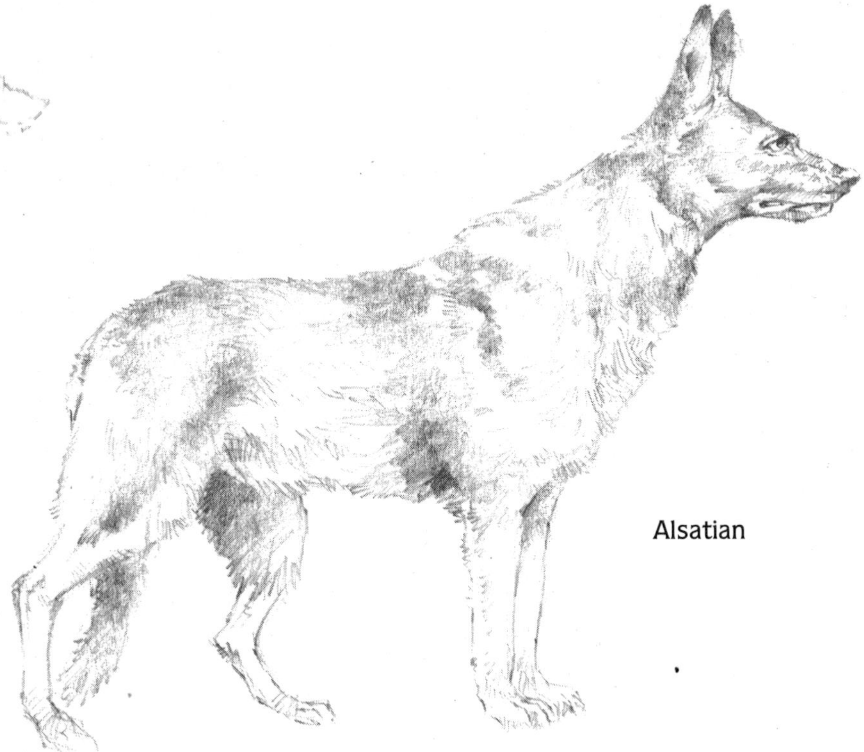

Alsatian

A domestic and easily found animal is always the most suitable subject for the beginners. You can see it whenever you want and correct your drawing. Instead of using basic shapes, we have placed the primary drawing in direct and short, thin strokes.

Labrador

Dogs are one of the animals which can provide you a good variety in shape, size and skin texture. Try to grasp the basić body shape and the posture first and then if you are satisfied with the accuracy, add the shades and details.

Fox Terrier

Texture of the skin and the type of fur is very important in animal drawing. Use smooth and mixed strokes for the Dog like the small one given below and concentrated, directional lines for the creatures who have long fur.

Mexican Dog

This is the heaviest Dog and has a very stout body. Drawing should be corresponding to the real body structure of the animal concerned. After sketching it accurately we have added the dark shades on the main parts in bold strokes, and then an overall re-drawing of the whole picture but in detail finished the brute animal.

Funny thing about this dog is the foolish look it has on its face. Try to see the interesting things in a picture.

St. Bernard

The Cat on the opposite page is finished in a photogenic way and the one below has got attention on the head only. See the number of strokes and the percentage of finishing on both pictures. This difference is called the approach towards a drawing.

Sometimes we use only the necessary lines while on some pictures, a lot of details. It all depends on how we like our sketch to look like, whether it is a suggestive sketch with a few lines or a fully detailed drawing like the one given on the opposite page.

Cat

Cat

Cow

Camels are big animals who have an awkward type of body structure.

Start with the circle of the body and add the head and then the neck. Re-draw the whole picture as per the real creature in detail.

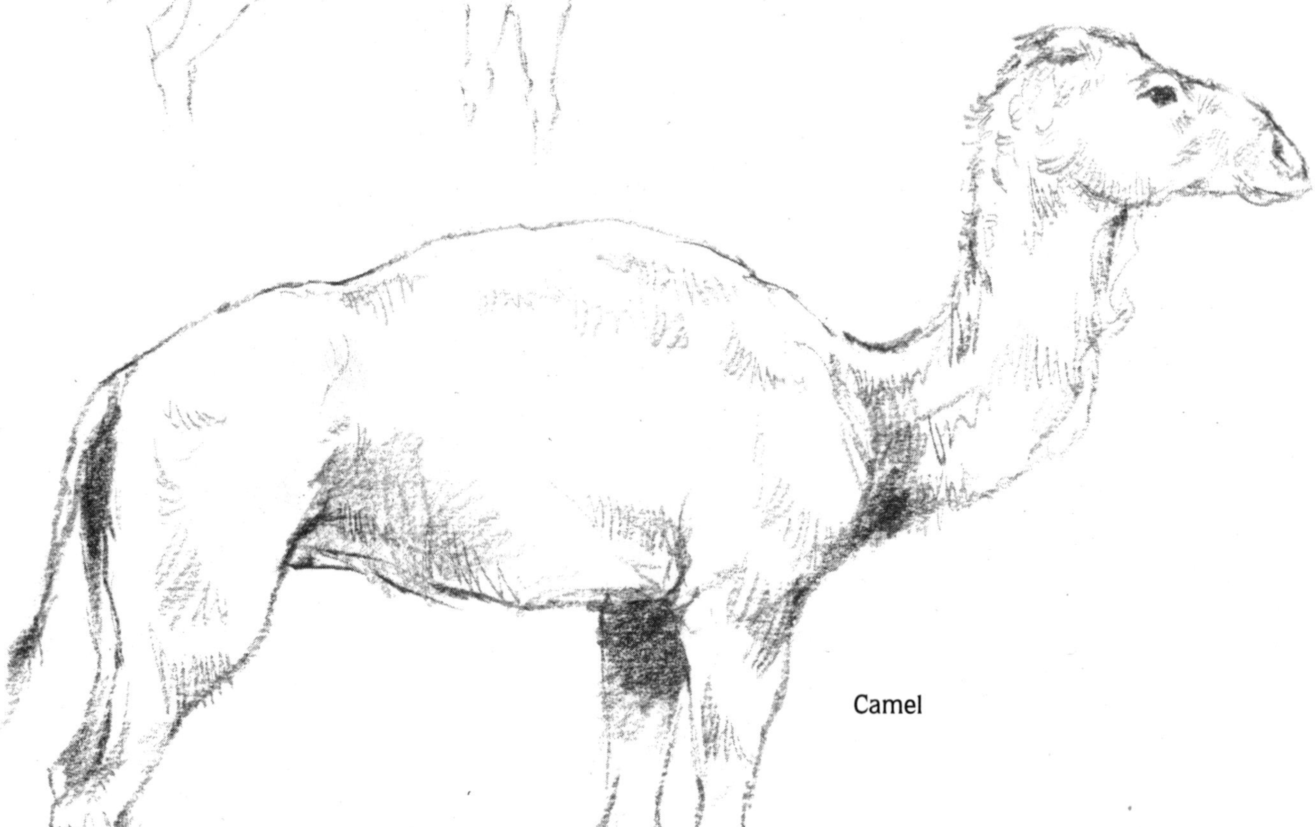

Camel

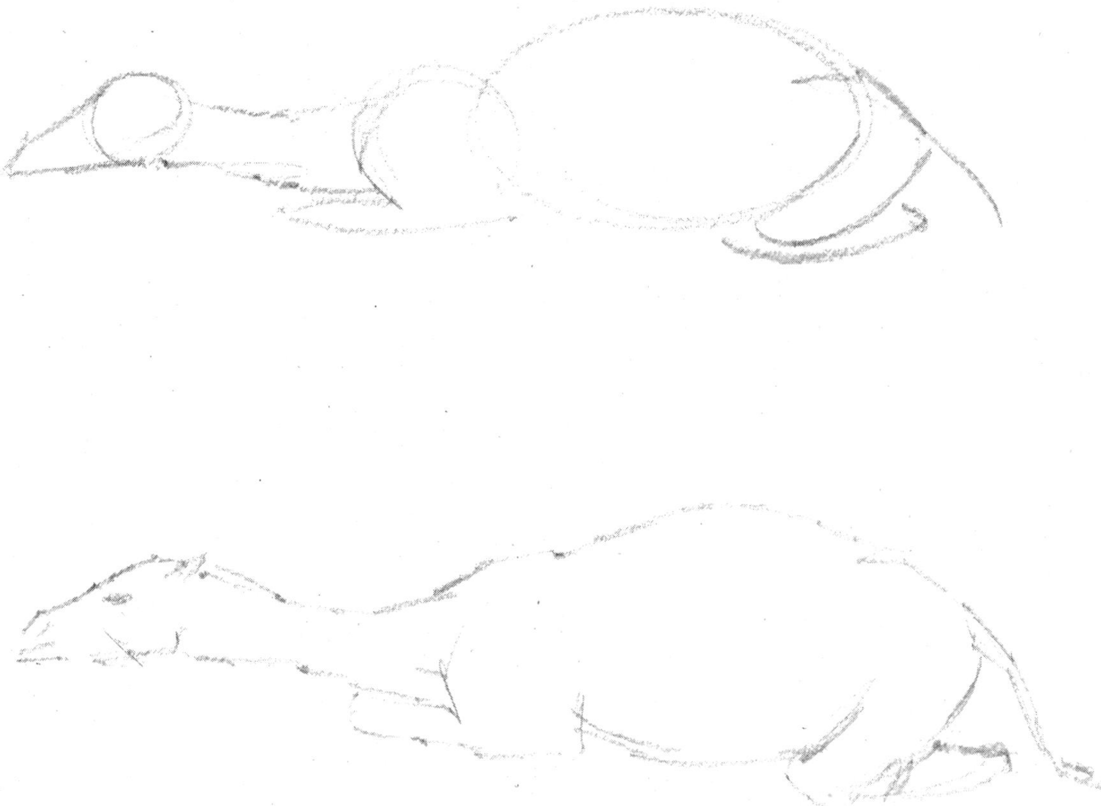

Camel

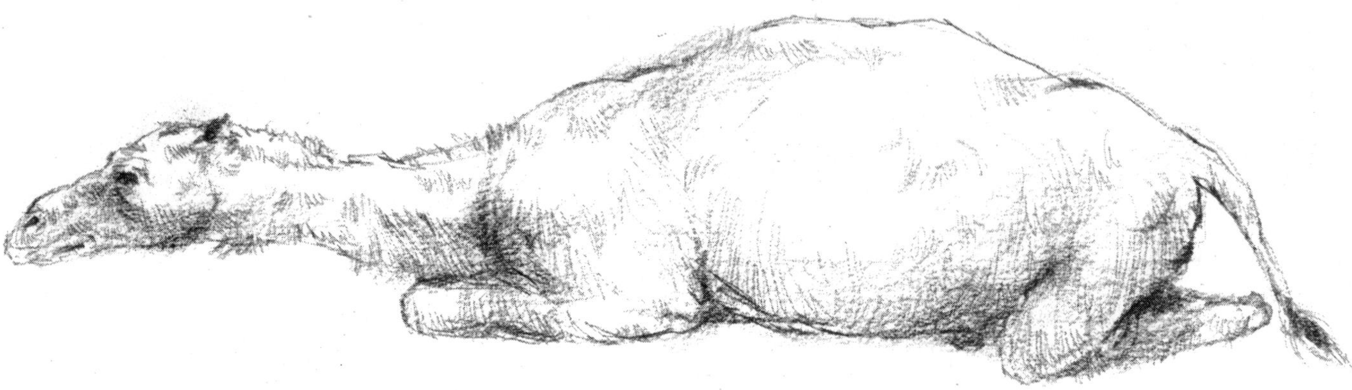

Raccoon

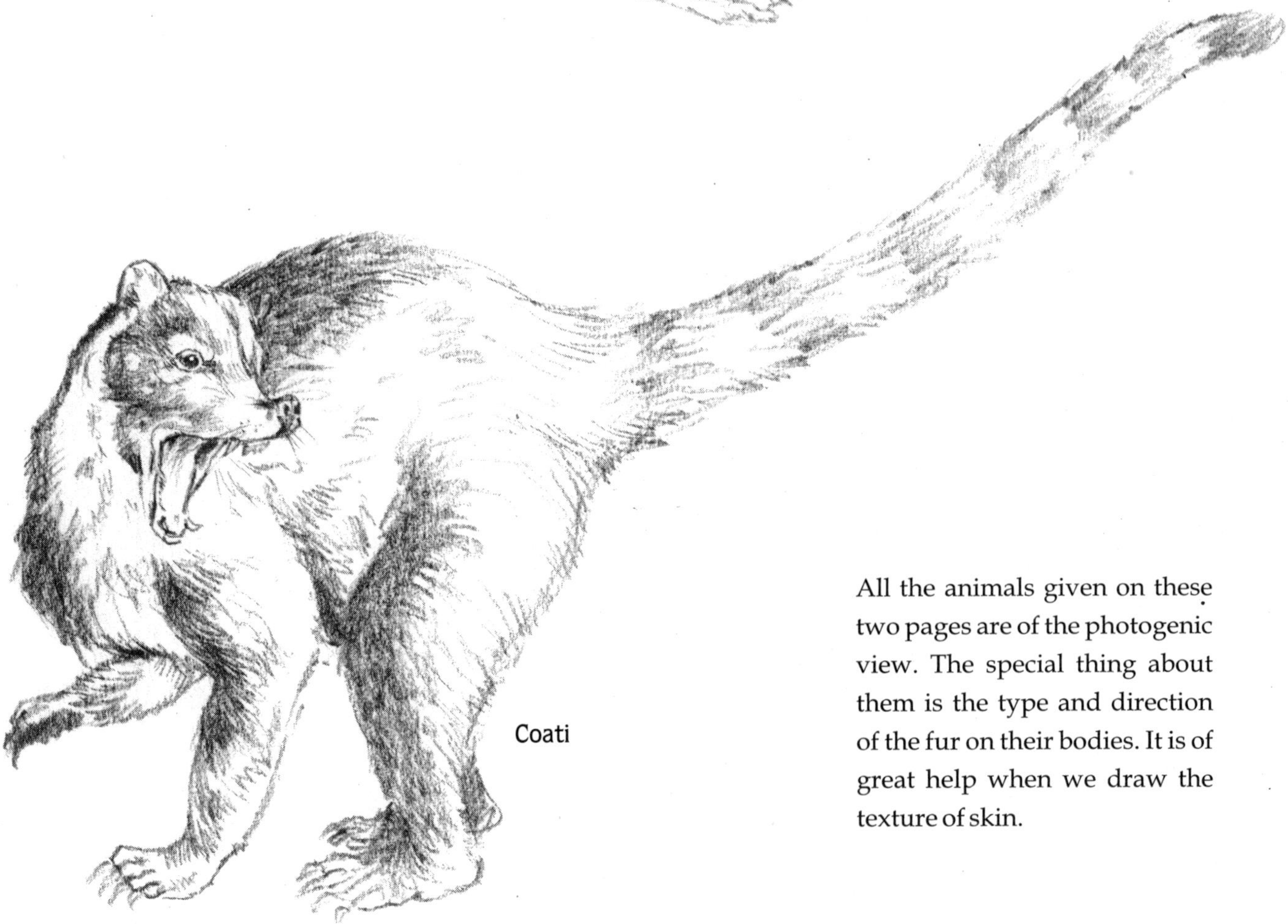

Coati

All the animals given on these two pages are of the photogenic view. The special thing about them is the type and direction of the fur on their bodies. It is of great help when we draw the texture of skin.

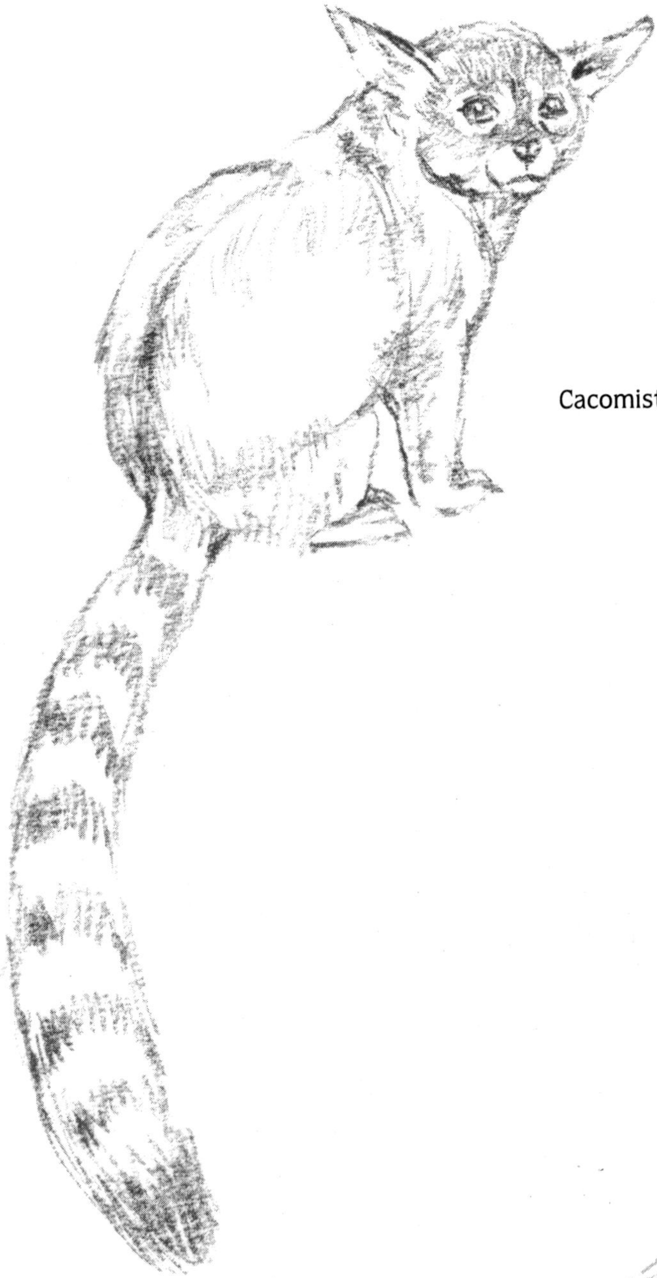

Cacomistle

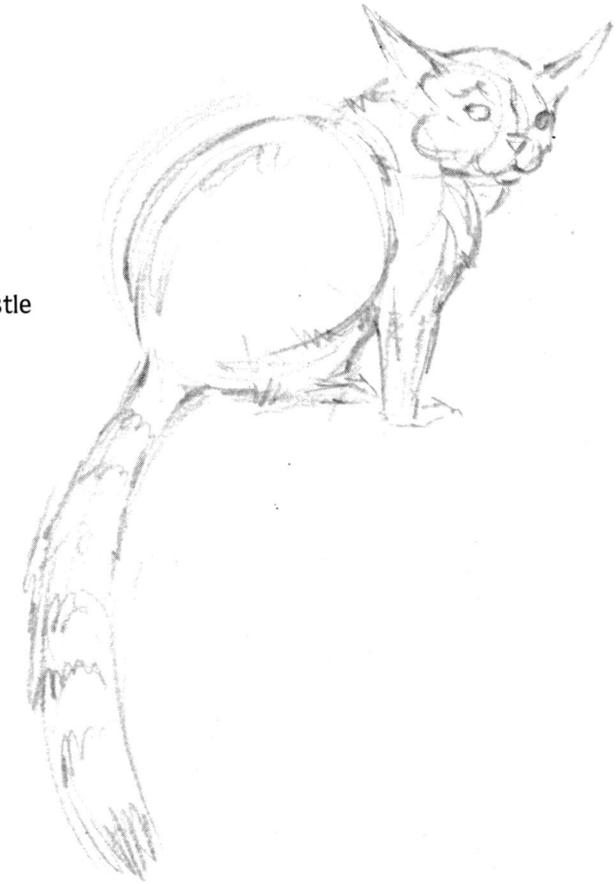

Lion

Wildebeest

Tiger

Elephant

Gorilla

Tiger

Tigers

Animals like Tiger and Zebra do not need much detail to define their body curvatures. You just have to know the pattern of their stripes. See the drawings on these pages and you will find that the outline of the animal is done carefully. The stripes have done the rest.

Knowledge of anatomy of the animal concerned becomes invaluable when you draw the picture in a few lines and in different postures.

Always start the drawing with basic shapes. It will help you in placing your animal as you like. Then draw the creature keeping in mind the bone and muscular structure. Your Tiger should be identifiable now. Add the detail on the face or whatever your point of interest is, and stripes to the body. Make the important lines more dark and define the curvature by subtle shades.

Tigers

Tiger

Carefully see the sketches given on this page and try to understand the motive behind each of them. The Tiger on top has nothing but stripes and some details on the face. The one below has a totally different approach. The first one is a quick study of a certain posture where you do not need much detail for your purpose. The second one is a detail study for painting where you have to decide beforehand how the different parts of the animal should look like. Also note the change in the facial expression between this one and the tiger on the next page. Both have their mouth wide open but the mood is not the same.

Leopard is one of the most beautiful animals of the Indian jungles but is also the most cunning and dangerous predator. Draw it as if you are drawing a big cat, then simply add the circular black patches. Now add the necessary details around the pre-decided focal point.

Leopard

Jaguar is the American cousin of the Indian Leopard. The basic difference between them is that the Jaguar is heavier and has a smoother skin. The black patches are bigger in size but less dark in tone. Simply follow the steps given here and you will see the difference yourself.

Jaguar

Never depart from the habit of starting a drawing with very simple geometrical shapes. The picture given below is somewhat a modified line drawing of circular basic shapes. Here we have combined the circular and conical shapes. The weight in dark shades should be added only at a few areas that you want to appear important.

Tapir

Tapir

Things which are near you will be bigger than the objects placed away from you. See the sketch given here.

The head of the Tapir is drawn in the same fashion. The body parts away from the head are smaller and shorter in proportion. The darkest areas are around the eyes and the nose.

As you grow more confident with direct drawing of an animal, try this Giant Panda. The hairy body of this animal is of relatively awkward proportion. You have to draw every part accurately and individually.

Giant Panda

After drawing the animal as given on the opposite page, start finishing the head first. The eyes, nose and mouth should be the point of interest. As you move away from it on to the other parts, keep reducing the details. Use bold strokes and also the tone should be lighter on the whitish parts.

Loris

Loris is a small and shy animal. The technique is to define the eyes and nose in detail as much as you can. The other sections are just there to create a body and support those beautiful, big and curious eyes. Keep the strokes small and concentrate on the eyes. The body should be drawn in bold and separate lines. The direction of these strokes is very important as it defines the texture of the fur.

Loris

Know Your Subject

You should not only know the anatomical features of your subject but also the habits and various postures in which it moves around. This knowledge is the key to an excellent sketch.

See the Bear above and the finished picture of it in a certain posture.

The other drawing of it in minimum lines below the first one is an example of how this knowledge can help you achieve a good drawing with minimum efforts.

Bear

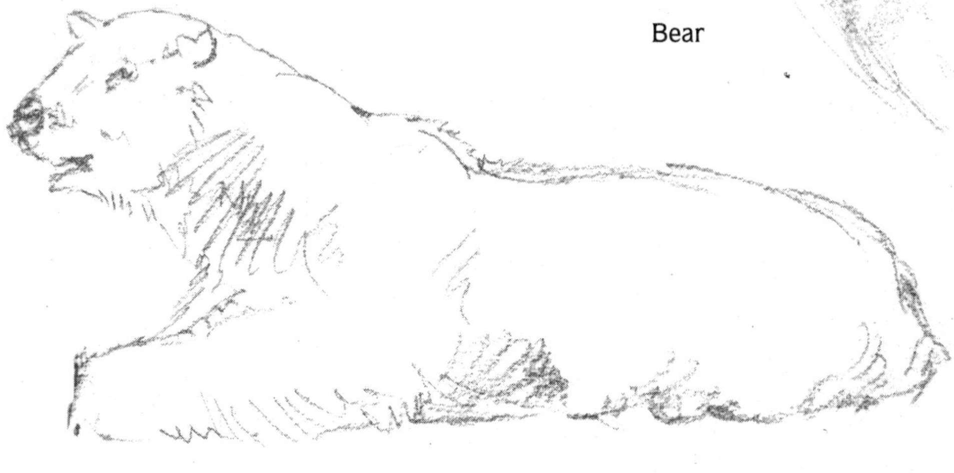

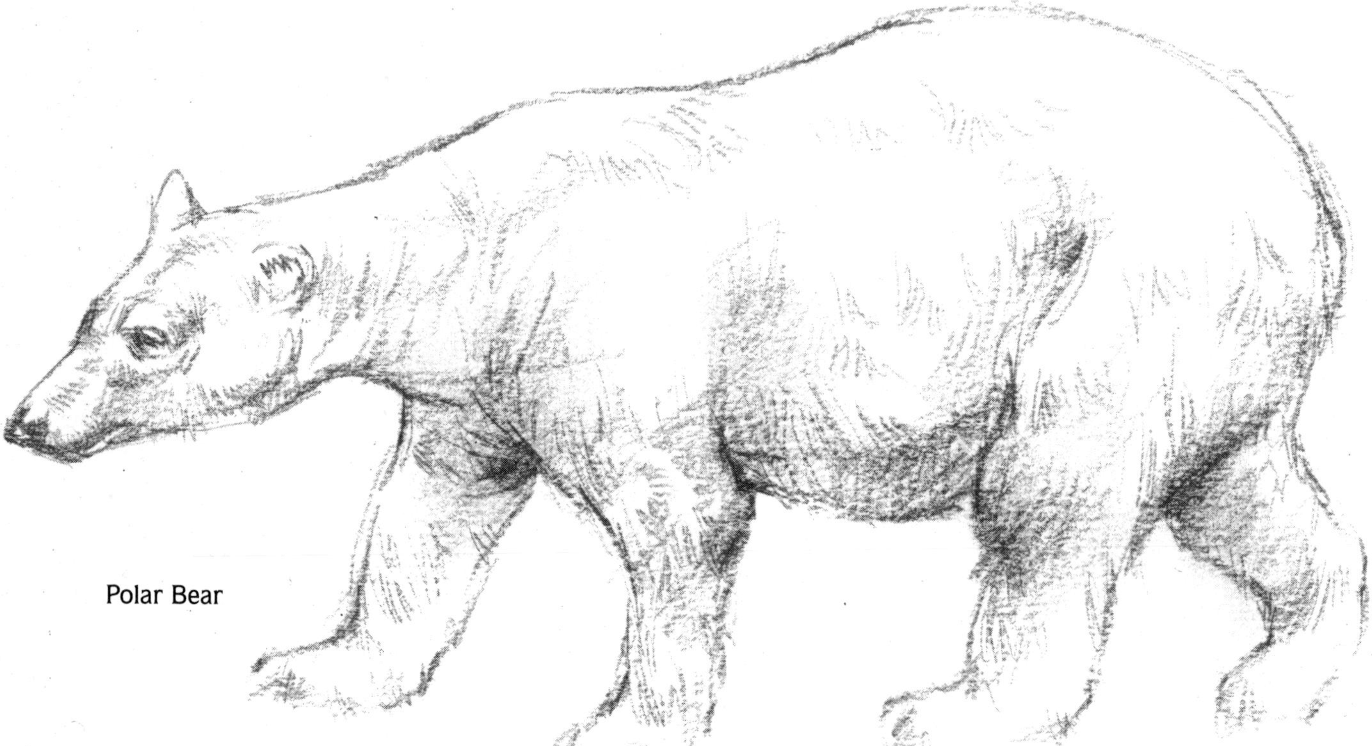

Polar Bear

Brown Bear

If you look carefully at the different pictures of various type of Bears given on these two pages, you will know what we mean by 'knowing' your subject.

The Polar Bear on the opposite page has a somewhat long body shape while the Brown Bear on this page is of a more compact and round-shaped body. The other important thing is the type and direction of the fur on both the animals.

Wolf

Wolf

The Wolf is one of our favourite animals for sketching. The common Wolf given alongside provides a good opportunity to study and draw the long fur on its body.

The Snow Wolf above, however, presents a challenge because you cannot use much shades, and have to rely on the direction and length of the stroke. Would you now like to draw it?

Pine Marten

Small creatures like these two are most suitable for pleasure sketching. You don't have to worry much about the exact line drawing and can have fun. The only thing which will keep you busy is the face and eyes as they are the key to show their curious nature.

Raccoon

We generally miss the most easily available animals around us. Rats are very good subjects for learning animal drawing. You may not be able to sell a painting of Rats but see the sketches given here.

The big and hairy Rat on the right side is finished in maximum and short lines whereas the small Rat below it has few lines with concentration of shades on eyes, ears and the joint of the tail only.

Rats

Interplay of the source of light and the body shape of the creature present an interesting result as you can see on the Rat given here on this page. Simply follow the steps and see the amazing results you can achieve.

Rat

Kangaroo

The most common and difficult problem you can face when drawing big animals is to put weight on their bodies.

The technique is to use lots of bold and long strokes. Try it on this Kangaroo.

Kangaroo

A very strong light is falling on the face and body of this Rhino. After sketching the outline add the darkest shades and shadows first. The details in middle and light tone will finish the picture.

Rhino

Rhino

Rhino

Rhino's Head

Drawings, difficulties and the will to overcome it will never end. You keep embarking on new journeys as you reach the previous targets. So good luck to all of you and keep drawing...........

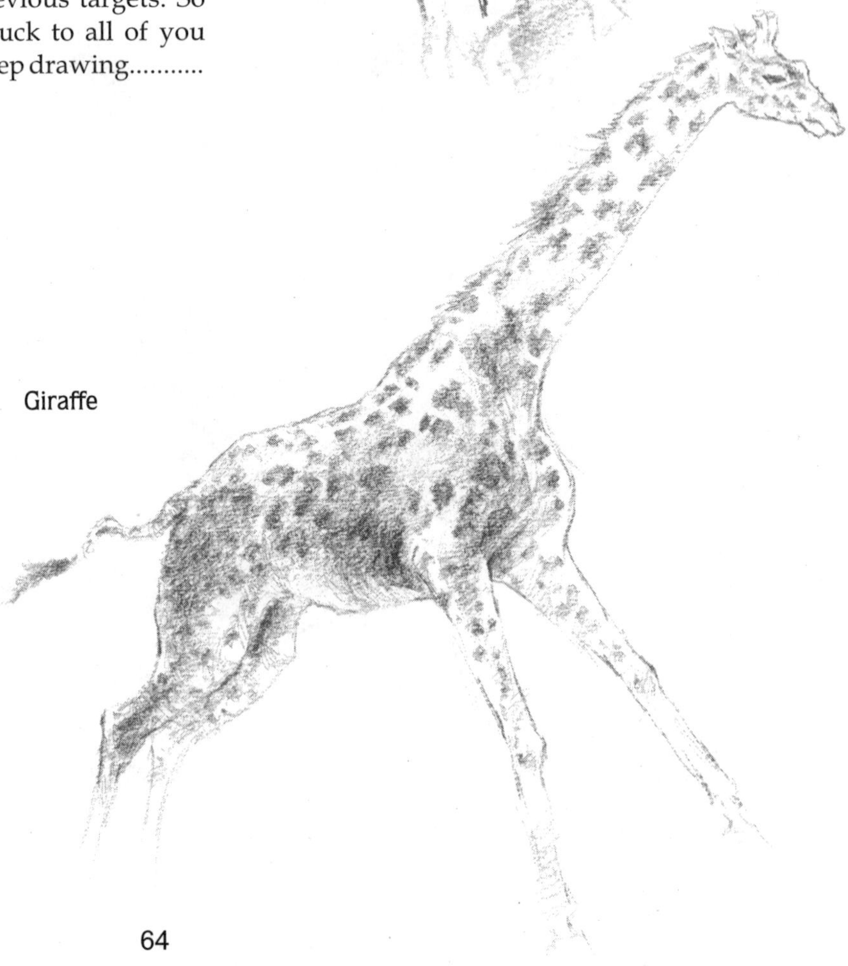

Giraffe